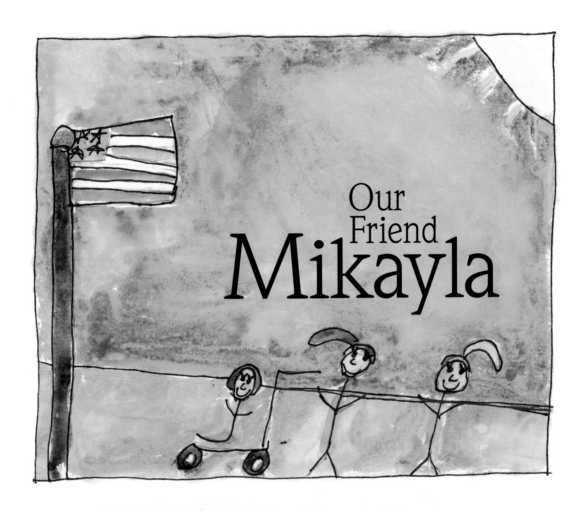

Our Friend Mikayla

Written and Illustrated by Mikayla's Third-Grade Classmates

at Lower Nazareth Elementary School
in Nazareth, Pennsylvania

Mikayla is my sister and I have never known any different than including her and treating her as if she didn't have a disability. If everybody learned to accept all people, our world would be a friendlier place for everyone to enjoy. Our community has made great strides in including everybody but progress can always be made. I think that the children in our community have been more accepting of Mikayla than adults have. My hope is that after kids read and enjoy this book, they will teach their parents how to accept as they have learned from *Our Friend Mikayla*. Living life with a sister with a disability might be difficult at times, but I wouldn't have it any other way. Mikayla inspires me to live life at its fullest. My sister has a great life and I am so glad to be a part of it each and every day.

~ *Lauren (Mikayla's younger sister)*

Seven years after meeting Mikayla, I am so glad to be good friends with her and her family. From spending so much time with them, I have learned how to become more comfortable around people with disabilities, for which I am truly grateful. Many people often ask me, "Why is inclusion so important?" At first when I tried to answer this question, I found myself at a loss for words. After repeatedly being asked over time, I felt that I finally found the right response that fit perfectly: "I would not like people to exclude me, so I feel that it is just the right thing to do." I encourage other children and adults to share the message of inclusion in order to make a difference in their community just like we did in ours.

~ *Logan (Mikayla's long-time friend and former third-grade classmate)*

We dedicate
this book
to all people
with disabilities
and their friends.

Mikayla's Voice
PO Box 232, Nazareth, PA 18064
www.mikaylasvoice.org
610.746.2323

ISBN: 978-0-578-06305-8

Edited by Kimberly Resh (Mikayla's mom)
Book design by Rea Kaschak (Mikayla's aunt)

Third Edition, 2015

Mikayla is a girl in our third-grade class.

She is in a wheelchair

and has a lot of disabilities.

But that does not mean

we cannot be friends.

Mikayla needs a ramp to help her

get in and out of her mom's mini-van.

When our class goes on a field trip,

she uses a school bus with a special lift

that works like an elevator.

Mikayla rides in her wheelchair

up the ramp or lift

to get in the mini-van or bus.

She stays in her wheelchair for the ride,

but she still uses a seat belt!

Mikayla can't eat with her mouth

so she has a tube that goes right into her belly.

Her mom feeds her special milk through her tube.

She can still taste things like lollipops,

and her favorite treat is cotton candy.

Mikayla can't hear very well,

but she can hear us.

We love talking to her.

She can't see very well,

but she can see bright colors.

She can see red and yellow the best.

We use bright-colored markers and crayons

to color pictures for her.

Mikayla has "brain damage."

Before she was born,

when Mikayla was still in her mom's belly,

she didn't get enough air.

Because she didn't get enough oxygen to her brain,

her brain was injured.

Her brain doesn't send the right messages

to her legs, her arms,

and the other parts of her body she can't use.

That is why she can't walk or talk

and has trouble seeing and hearing.

When we first saw Mikayla,

we were surprised because we never had

a kid in our school in a wheelchair.

Most of us stared at her

because we didn't know what had happened.

We wanted to know what was wrong with Mikayla.

We had never met a kid with a disability.

We felt shy.

Most of us were also a little afraid

when we first met her.

We felt scared because

we thought Mikayla was different

and not like a "normal" kid.

We were afraid of what she had.

One of us even thought it was contagious,

but we learned it's not.

There is nothing to be scared of.

We felt bad for Mikayla

because she has brain damage

and is in a wheelchair.

We didn't know how to talk to her.

We thought she would not be able to

play games or sports with us.

We had no clue how to be Mikayla's friend.

But now we know.

It's much easier than we thought.

On Mikayla's first day of third grade,

her mom came in and told us about her.

She answered all our questions.

When we thought of new questions,

we asked our teachers.

We also asked other kids

who had known Mikayla before.

After a few weeks, we got used to Mikayla.

We weren't scared anymore because

we learned there is nothing to be afraid of.

We felt happy because we had never had

a friend with disabilities.

Now we do.

Mikayla is our friend.

We help push her to class.

We sit with Mikayla at lunch and talk to her.

At recess we push her in her special swing.

23

Kids with disabilities like to do

the same things we do.

Mikayla likes to listen to music.

She watches "American Idol" with her family.

She is a Clay Aiken fan.

Last summer she even saw Clay in concert!

Mikayla goes to the mall

and shops at the same stores we do.

She wears the same kinds of clothes,

and she might even get her ears pierced.

We think she should!

Mikayla can even do some sports.

She roller-skates at "Skateaway."

She uses her wheelchair to skate

because she has wheels on the bottom of it.

Someone just has to push her around.

Mikayla is a cheerleader.

She likes to cheer.

Every game she wears her uniform
and brings her pom-poms.
The other girls hold her hands
and help her shake them.
She has signs on her wheelchair that say
"Go Wildcats!" and stuff like that.

Mikayla goes bowling.

Instead of throwing the ball,

she drops the ball down a special ramp.

Someone helps her push the ball off.

The ball will roll all the way down

to hit the bowling pins.

In gym class,

she can use the bowling ramp

to pitch when we play kickball.

It was our idea to have Mikayla be the pitcher.

35

Mikayla talks to us by hitting her "switch."

Her switch is a button you put on her wheelchair.

Whenever she turns her head to hit it,

the switch controls whatever it is hooked up to.

She uses her switch to talk

by playing a recorded message.

Mikayla has to practice hitting her switch

so it gets easier for her.

Mikayla can work almost anything with her switch.

She has a special spinner with all our names on it.

By using her switch, Mikayla spins the spinner

to pick which of us will be her helper for the day.

She uses her switch to play games,

like the math bingo game.

By hitting her switch to make a fan work,

Mikayla can blow out the candles on her birthday cake.

She also uses her switch to cook.

Her sister holds the mixer

while Mikayla powers it with her switch.

From Mikayla, we've learned that

people with disabilities aren't really different.

Mikayla is no different from anyone else.

She does things in a special way,

but she can do just about everything we can.

Now that we know more about Mikayla,

we feel silly that we were afraid of her.

She is just like us.

We are glad Mikayla can do things we can

and are happy we made a new friend.

We hope Mikayla is in our class again.

If we meet someone who doesn't know Mikayla,

we will introduce her.

We will tell them what happened to Mikayla

and explain about her disabilities.

Even if we have to explain over and over again, we will…

because they might be afraid

just like we were when we met her.

We will tell other kids not to be scared,

that Mikayla is nice,

and it's fun to have her as a friend.

It doesn't matter if your friend

is in a wheelchair.

Their disabilities don't mean

you cannot be friends.

Having a friend with a disability is cool.

Children have always been the most accepting of Mikayla's disabilities and the least afraid to ask questions. Understanding is the key to acceptance so I have always given them honest, but sometimes overly complicated answers. Many years ago when a young child asked about Mikayla's feeding tube, Lauren (Mikayla's then three-year-old sister) merely explained, "Mommy feeds Mikayla special milk with a special tube." The boy was clearly satisfied while I would have given too much information, probably leaving the child confused. Being the same age as the child who posed the question, Lauren was able to give just the right answer for his developmental level and understanding. Children are sometimes the best teachers.

Each year, in appreciation for our school's efforts, we purchased books on diversity and disability to donate to the school library. As I searched for new and different books on this topic, with the exception of publications for siblings, I did not find a children's book about disability written by kids. Encouraged by my belief that kids often offer the best explanations for other children, I asked Mikayla's principal and teacher to let me help Mikayla's class write and illustrate a book about having a friend with a disability. Having met her just two years earlier, Mikayla's third-grade classmates knew what it was like to meet and become friends with someone with multiple disabilities. Through their book, Mikayla's friends let other children know it's okay to be afraid when you first meet someone with a disability, but "there is nothing to be scared of." *Our Friend Mikayla* is a valuable tool for teachers and parents who wish to help kids who may be afraid or intimidated upon meeting a disabled child in their school or community. It is an honest and beautiful story about friendship that should be shared with children of all ages.

Motivated by the success of *Our Friend Mikayla*, we started a 501(c)(3) non-profit organization to inspire kids of all abilities to share the message of inclusion. An acronym for the **V**oice **O**f **I**nclusion for **C**hildren **E**verywhere, **Mikayla's Voice** helps children take on projects through which they can share the value and benefits of inclusion. Our projects are as diverse and creative as the kids who create them. We empower children by supporting their ideas, funding their projects, and finding ways to present their work to make certain their message is heard. Through increased inclusive practices in our schools and communities, this generation of children has been blessed with greater appreciation for and friendships with children with disabilities. It is important to help them share the benefits of inclusion so this trend may continue to grow.

~ *Kimberly (Mikayla's proud mom)*

Inspiring kids of all abilities to share the message of inclusion...

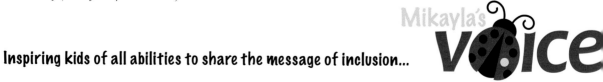